Making Music

Banging

Angela Aylmore

Raintree

Chicago, Illinois

© 2006 Raintree
Published by Raintree, a division of Reed Elsevier, Inc.
Chicago, Illinois
Customer Service 888-363-4266
Visit our website at www.raintreelibrary.com

Printed and bound by South China Printing Company.
10 09 08 07 06
10 9 8 7 6 5 4 3 2 1

Library of Congress Cataloging-in-Publication Data:

Aylmore, Angela.
   Banging / Angela Aylmore.
      p. cm. -- (Making music)
   Includes index.
   ISBN 1-4109-1604-9 (library binding-hardcover) -- ISBN 1-4109-1609-X
(pbk.) 1. Percussion instruments--Juvenile literature. I. Title. II. Series:
Aylmore, Angela. Making music.
   ML1030.A95 2005
   786.8'19--dc22

                              2005002423

Acknowledgments
The publishers would like to thank the following for permission to reproduce photographs:
Alamy p. **15**; Corbis pp. **4b**, **5a**, **6**, **18**; Harcourt Education pp. **14** (Gareth Boden), **4a**, **5b** (Trevor Clifford), **13** (Peter Evans), **18** (Christ Honeywell), **7**, **8**, **9**, **10**, **11**, **12**, **16**, **17**, **19**, **20**, **21**, **22-23** (Tudor Photography).

Cover photograph of a girl playing a drum, reproduced with permission of Harcourt Education/Tudor Photography.

Every effort has been made to contact copyright holders of any material reproduced in this book. Any omissions will be rectified in subsequent printings if notice is given to the publishers.

Some words are shown in bold, **like this**. You can find out what they mean by looking in the glossary on page 24.

2

Contents

Let's Make Music!

We can make **music** by banging!

Ravi **bangs** the drum.

Crash go the cymbals!

4

Tom hits his xylophone.

The triangle goes **ting ting!**

5

Play the Drum

Can you play the drum?

Bang it hard.
Make it loud.

Bang!

Make Your Own

Can you make a drum?

My drum is made from an old box.

Boom!

Can you play a pan?

Bang

Slow, slow. Faster and faster.

13

What Are They?

These drums are from Indonesia.
They are called bonang.

A bonang sounds like a gong.

Play the Cymbals

Bang the cymbals together!

Crash!

16

Now, tap them gently.

Ping

Keep in Time

click-clack

castanets

The castanets click-clack.

The dancer's feet tip-tap.

tip-tap

18

Listen Carefully

What can you hear?

ting

triangle

maracas

violin

recorder

What makes that sound?

It's a triangle!

Let's all play together!

ting

clip-clop

Glossary

bang   hit something and make a sound
music   a mixture of sounds to express an idea or emotion
note   a specific single sound, which can be written

Index

Notes for Adults

Making Music provides children with an opportunity to think about sound and the different ways instruments can be played to create music. The concepts of volume, rhythm, speed, and pitch are introduced, and children are encouraged to think about how controlling their movements can create different sounds when they play instruments.

This book explores the different ways of creating music by banging. It includes a range of instruments, some with pitch and some without, and looks at different ways that instruments can be hit to create different sounds, by using sticks or hands, by hitting hard or tapping gently, and by banging quickly or slowly.

Follow-up Activities

• With their eyes closed, ask the children to identify the instruments that you play.

• Can the children use their instruments to represent different feelings and emotions? For example, quick high notes on the xylophone might express being 'happy', while slow low notes might express being 'sad'.